DATE DUE

OCT 0 8 2002		
NOV 0 4 2002		
NOV 0 6 2004		

Demco, Inc. 38-293

Plank House

Written by
Dolores A. Dyer

Illustrated by
Kimberly L. Dawson Kurnizki

The Rourke Book Company, Inc.
Vero Beach, Florida 32964

2

Library of Congress Cataloging-in-Publication Data

Dyer, Dolores A. (Dolores Anna)
  Plank house / Dolores A. Dyer.
    p. cm. — (Native American homes)
  Includes index.
  ISBN 1-55916-248-1
  1. Indians of North America—Dwellings—Northwest, Pacific—Juvenile literature. 2. Indian architecture—Northwest, Pacific—Juvenile literature. I. Title. II. Series.

E78.N77 D84 2000
728'.089'970795—dc21

                                                    00–025459

Printed in the USA

Contents

The Northwest Coast 4

The People of the Northwest. 6

Types of Plank Houses 8

Gathering the Wood. 12

Building a Plank House 16

Inside the House. 20

Plank House Villages 22

Ceremonies 24

Plank Houses Today 26

Make a Model Plank House. 28

Glossary 30

Further Reading. 31

Suggested Web Sites 31

Index 32

The Northwest Coast

The Pacific Northwest begins in northern California. It includes western Oregon and Washington in the United States and reaches north through British Columbia, Canada, up to Alaska. It goes along the Pacific Ocean for 1,200 miles (1900 kilometers). A lot of rain falls here. The average amount is 80 inches (200 centimeters) in a year.

The rain fills the Northwest's many rivers and streams. It also waters forests of huge cedar, spruce, and hemlock trees. Cedar trees were especially prized by the Native Americans who lived in the Northwest.

Many animals live in the rivers and forests. Fish fill the rivers. Deer, elk, bears, and birds live in the forests. Fruits and berries also grow in the forests and clearings. Along the seashore are oysters, and fish and whales swim in the ocean. All these animals and plants provided plenty of food for the tribes of the Northwest.

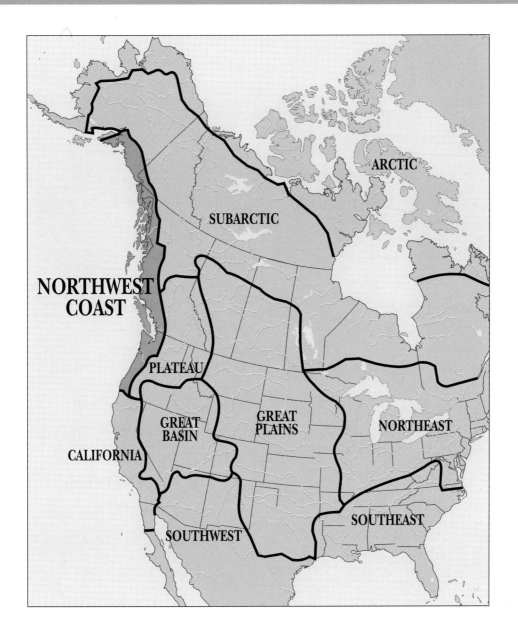

The temperature here is comfortable, not very hot or freezing cold. It is rainy for about eight or nine months of the year, from the fall to the spring. Summers are sunny and pleasant.

The People of the Northwest

Many different Native American tribes lived in the Pacific Northwest. Each *tribe* had its own customs, language, and style of house. The Salish, Chinook, and Tillamook lived in the south. The Kwakiutl, Bella Coola, and Nootka lived in the central section. The Tlingit, Haida, and Tsimshian lived in the north. All these people lived in the Northwest for thousands of years.

Because food was easy to get, the people did not have to spend all their time meeting their basic needs. They had time to decorate their clothing, tools, boats, and buildings with bold designs of animals and people. The designs showed stories from the history of the tribe and pictured characters from myths.

The chief was the most respected person of the village. Next in line were skilled craftspeople, then regular workers, hunters, and fishermen. Some tribes also had slaves. These were members of other tribes who had been captured. Slaves were forced to work very hard, but they lived in the same houses as the members of the tribe.

Types of Plank Houses

The Native Americans of the Pacific Northwest lived in plank houses before Europeans moved into the area more than 100 years ago. A plank is a big, flat piece of wood like a thick board. The planks used in plank houses might be 20 feet (6 meters) long, 1 or 2 feet (0.3 to 0.6 meter) wide, and anywhere from 2 to 5 inches (5 to 13 centimeters) thick. The frame of the house was built using huge logs. The walls and roof were then covered with planks.

Plank houses were very large. Some were almost square, with sides 40 to 60 feet (12 to 18 meters) long. Others were shaped like rectangles. One famous plank house was 75 feet by 90 feet (23 by 27 meters), about one-third as long as a football field and almost half as wide. Several families lived in each house. As many as 60 to 100 people might live in one large house.

All the tribes in the Pacific Northwest built plank houses, but different tribes built different types. Differences included the shape of the house, how it was built, and the special designs used to decorate the house. The tribes of the south built long and narrow plank houses with flat roofs. Their houses were plain and undecorated.

The central tribes built houses with slanted roofs. They often painted huge murals on the front walls of their houses. The door into the house might be through the painted mouth of a fierce-looking creature.

Craftsmen from the northern tribes were famous for their wood-carving skills. It was very important to have a well-built house in this colder climate. Inside these houses, the posts and roof beams sometimes had designs carved into them.

Totem poles stood in front of northern plank houses. Sometimes the poles were attached to the houses.

The northern houses were known for their *totem* poles. Totem poles stood at the entrances to houses or villages. A totem pole is a single tall log that is carved with special designs. Totem poles could be two or three times taller than the houses. Sometimes a totem pole was connected to the front of a plank house. A person had to walk through a hole in the totem pole to go into the house.

Gathering the Wood

A chief or other wealthy person in the village decided when a new plank house needed to be built. Many people had to work hard to build the house. Some gathered the wood; others cleared the land. Expert builders did many of the jobs. People with special skills carved wood for making decorative poles. At every step along the way, the chief performed ceremonies, had feasts, and paid the builders with gifts such as blankets.

The first step was to gather the wood. Cedar, spruce, and hemlock trees were used. Cedar was the best wood for Northwest Coast houses for several reasons. First, cedar can be split into flat planks with simple tools. Second, it is easy to carve. Third, it has natural oils that keep it from rotting in the wet weather. Cedar trees also had other uses. The soft inner bark was woven into mats, cloth, and rope.

A group of men and boys went into the forest looking for the best cedar trees. When they found a good tree, they held a ceremony. They asked the tree for permission to use it and thanked the tree.

One man climbed the tree and tied a rope near the top. Then the men chipped all around the base with stone hammers and chisels to weaken the tree. Sometimes they lit a small fire at the bottom of the tree to make the bark and wood easier to chip out. They put a ring of mud above the fire to keep the fire from burning the whole tree. When they had weakened the base of the tree enough, they pulled it down with the rope.

The men and boys cut off its branches and bark. Then they pounded pointed pieces of hard wood into the trunk to split it into planks. The planks were smoothed with a tool called an *adze*. The finished planks were bundled and dragged to the nearest river or to the ocean. The men towed the planks and logs back to their village behind their boats, called *canoes*.

Building a Plank House

After they brought the wood back to the village, the men measured the land where the house was going to be built. They cleared it of plants and rocks.

Sometimes workers dug the floor deeper than the ground level. A deep floor could have two or three levels going down like wide steps toward the center of the house. At the bottom, in the middle, the builders dug holes for cooking and heating fires.

Next, the men dug holes for the large logs or posts that would hold up the roof beams. It was hard work setting the heavy posts firmly in the holes. Then groups of men used ropes and logs to lift two long, thick logs onto the posts to make the main roof beams. They used thinner poles to build the frame of the roof. Then it was time to put the wood planks in place to form the walls and roof. Some tribes put the wall planks on up-and-down (vertically). Others ran the planks on their sides (horizontally) and tied them on with rope made of soft cedar bark.

Smoke holes were left in the roof. The holes were covered with loose planks that could be moved with a pole to let the smoke out. The houses had no windows.

Some plank houses were decorated with special designs or wood carvings. The Kwakiutl tribe painted fancy designs on the fronts of some of their houses. The paintings showed fish, bears, whales, or ravens. The design, or *crest*, belonged to the related families who lived in the house. People who were part of the bear clan, for example, would paint a bear design on their house. A *clan* is a group of related families.

The paintings on the front of the houses had important meanings to the clan that lived in the village.

The stories of the crests were a valuable part of the heritage of the tribe. These stories were told to each generation and were an important part of the group's ceremonies.

Inside the House

A plank house was so huge that many families could sleep in it. Each family had its own section. The sections were divided by thin walls that did not reach all the way to the roof.

Some plank houses had built-in sleeping platforms along the walls.

The best area was in the back, away from the door. The chief's family slept there. The other families had places around the walls, from the back around to the door in front. The cooking and heating fires were in the center. Most houses had dirt floors, but in some houses the floor was covered with wood planks.

The women cooked with pots and cooking boxes. To cook with a wood cooking box, a woman filled the box with water and fish. Then she added hot stones from the fire to boil the water and cook the food.

Bedding was kept against the walls of the house. Boxes and bags of stored food were stashed around the different levels. Racks of dried fish were kept overhead in the roof beams.

Plank House Villages

Native American villages in the Northwest were many different sizes. Some small villages had only a few plank houses. Larger towns had several rows of houses. The people built their villages along the ocean or a river's edge. The fronts of the houses always faced the water.

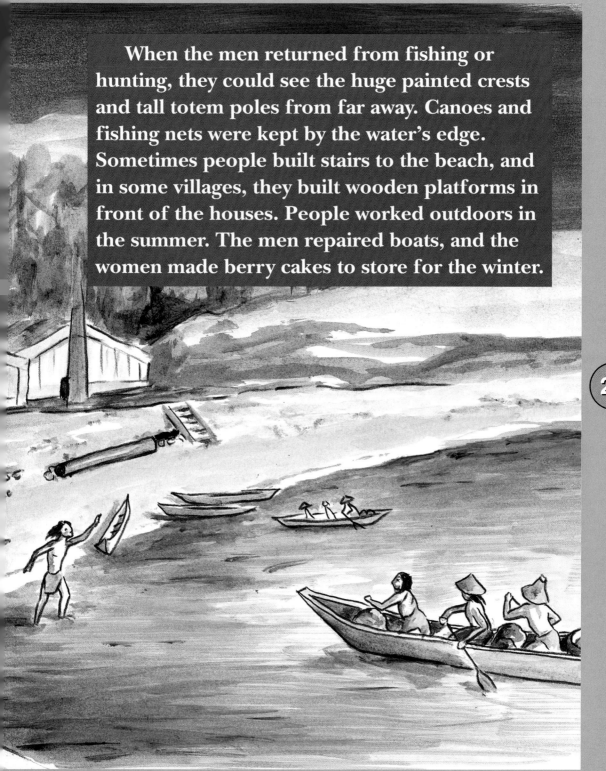

When the men returned from fishing or hunting, they could see the huge painted crests and tall totem poles from far away. Canoes and fishing nets were kept by the water's edge. Sometimes people built stairs to the beach, and in some villages, they built wooden platforms in front of the houses. People worked outdoors in the summer. The men repaired boats, and the women made berry cakes to store for the winter.

23

Ceremonies

In the winter, many ceremonies and feasts were held in the plank house village. Sometimes hundreds of people would gather in the largest house in the village. This house belonged to the village chief.

The people would see plays and dances that told the stories and legends of the tribe. Musicians played drums made from hollowed logs. Actors wore costumes and painted wooden masks. Some masks had moving parts that opened to reveal a mask inside the mask. Special magic effects were also used. Painted wood puppets would swing down from the ceiling on strings. Performers appeared and disappeared through hidden passages.

The *potlatch* was an important ceremony. A chief held a potlatch to show his wealth and power or to celebrate the building of a house. For a potlatch, the chief would gather his family's possessions. Then he would give them away. The more he gave away, the more important he was.

In a plank house in Alaska, modern dancers perform a traditional dance with Chilkat blankets.

Plank Houses Today

Many Native Americans still live along the Northwest Coast. They do not live in plank houses today. However, they have built copies of the large houses of long ago. Some are used as community centers for tribes.

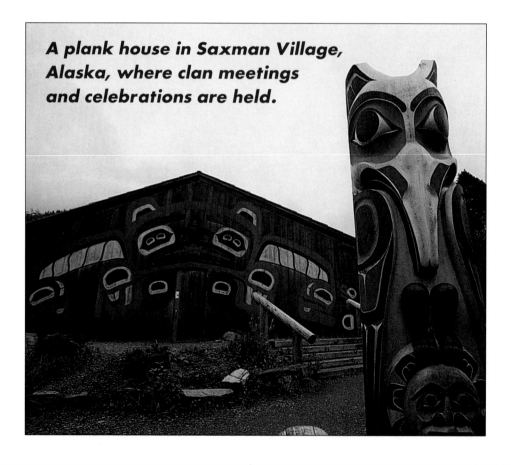

A plank house in Saxman Village, Alaska, where clan meetings and celebrations are held.

Here craftspeople carve totem poles, weave cedar-bark mats, and make canoes. They also perform ceremonies and dances to honor and remember their ancestors. Examples of these community centers are at Alert Bay, Skidegate, and K'SAN in British Columbia, Canada.

Many museums in the United States and Canada have information and exhibits on the Native Americans of the Northwest Coast. A few are the Burke Museum in Seattle, Washington, the Field Museum in Chicago, Illinois, and the American Museum of Natural History in New York City. In Quebec, Canada, the Canadian Museum of Civilization has a plank house on display.

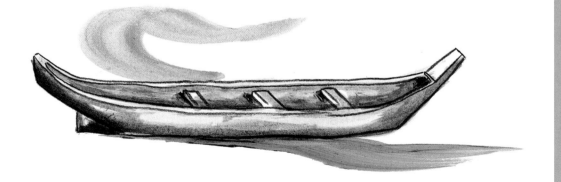

Make a Model Plank House

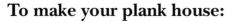

What you will need:

shoebox (no lid)
large piece of thin cardboard
craft sticks or other small,
    flat sticks
paints or colored markers
tape and glue
scissors

To make your plank house:

1. Trace the shape of one narrow end of the shoebox on the cardboard and add a triangle shape on top. Cut out the shape to form an end piece, then cut a second end piece the same shape.

2. Cut a cardboard rectangle the right size for the roof. Fold in half lengthwise.

3. Put the box on the floor, open side up. Glue sticks along the two long sides for the house's plank walls. When dry, turn the box over.

4. In one end piece, cut the door. Glue sticks on both end pieces. On the side with the door, draw or paint a Northwest Coast design. When dry, glue or tape both end pieces to the box.

5. Glue sticks to the roof piece. Let dry.

6. Place the roof over the box. Tape the roof in place.

Glossary

adze: a sharp tool made of wood and bone or metal; used to scrape the rough spots off a piece of wood to make it smooth.

canoe: a type of narrow boat that comes to a point at both the front and the back.

Chilkat blankets: fine blankets and robes woven by members of the Chilkat Tlingit people.

clan: a group of related families; clan members usually live in the same village, often in the same house.

crest: a design of an animal or plant that has meaning and represents the qualities of a clan.

potlatch: a ceremony in which a chief or other person of high status gives away his family's possessions to guests. The more gifts he gives away, the more important the person becomes.

totem: a symbol of an animal or plant that has special meaning for a tribe, clan, or family.

tribe: a large group made up of many families or clans; a tribe shares a common history and may be ruled by the same leader. The people of a tribe get their food, build their homes, and wear clothing in similar ways.

Further Reading

McConkey, Lois. *Sea and Cedar.* Seattle: Madrona Press, 1973.

Monroe, Jean Guard, and Ray A. Williamson. *First Houses: Native American Homes and Sacred Structures.* Boston: Houghton Mifflin, 1993.

Prentzas, G. S. *The Kwakiutl Indians.* New York: Chelsea House, 1993.

Press, Petra. *Indians of the Northwest: Traditions, history, Legends, and Life.* Milwaukee: Stevens, 2000.

Shemie, Bonnie. *Houses of Wood.* Chicago: Children's Press, 1992.

Suggested Web Sites

`Ksan Historical Village and Museum
<www.ksan.org>
Canadian Museum of Civilization
<www.civilization.ca>
Burke Museum of Natural History and Culture
<www.washington.edu/burkemuseum>
Field Museum of Natural History

Index

Alaska, 4
Bedding, 21
Bella Coola tribe, 6
British Columbia, 4
California, 4
Canoes, 15, 23, 27
Cedar trees, 4
Cedar wood, special
    qualities of, 12
Cedar-bark rope, 17
Ceremonies and feasts,
    24
Chinook tribe, 6
Clans, 18
Community centers, 26
Cooking, 21
Floors, 17
Food storage, 21
Haida tribe, 6
Hemlock trees, 12
Kwakiutl tribe, 6, 18

Masks, 24
Museums, 27
Nootka tribe, 6
Oregon, 4
Pacific Northwest, 4
Paintings, 18
Plank walls, 17
Planks, 8
Potlatch, 25
Puppets, 24
Salish tribe, 6
Slaves, 7
Smoke holes, 17
Spruce trees, 12
Tillamook tribe, 6
Tlingit tribe, 6
Totem poles, 11, 23, 27
Tsimshian tribe, 6
Villages, 22
Washington, 4